Horrid Heroes and Magic Monsters

Fiona Macdonald

is a department of the University of Oxford.
It furthers the University's objective of excellence in research, scholarship, and education by publishing worldwide in

Oxford New York
Auckland Cape Town Dar es Salaam Hong Kong Karachi
Kuala Lumpur Madrid Melbourne Mexico City Nairobi
New Delhi Shanghai Taipei Toronto

With offices in

Argentina Austria Brazil Chile Czech Republic France Greece
Guatemala Hungary Italy Japan Poland Portugal Singapore
South Korea Switzerland Thailand Turkey Ukraine Vietnam

First published 2007

British Library Cataloguing in Publication Data

Data available

ISBN: 978-0-19-846103-6

3 5 7 9 10 8 6 4 2

Printed in China

Paper used in the production of this book is a natural, recyclable product made from wood grown in sustainable forests. The manufacturing process conforms to the environmental regulations of the country of origin

Acknowledgements

The publisher would like to thank the following for permission to reproduce photographs: **p6** Erich Lessing /AKG – Images; **p7** C.M.Dixon/Ancient Art & Architecture Collection; **p8** Erich Lessing/ AKG – Images; **p10**t Visual Arts Library (London)/Alamy, **p10**b akg-images / Nimatallah/AKG – Images; 0**p11** Erich Lessing /AKG – Images; **p12** Kevin Fleming/Corbis UK Ltd.; **p14** Archaeological Museum Florence/Dagli Orti/Art Archive; **p15**l Araldo De Luca/Corbis UK Ltd., **p15**r Bibliothèque des Arts Décoratifs Paris/Dagli Orti/Art Archive; **p16** Erich Lessing /AKG – Images; **p17** C.M.Dixon/Ancient Art & Architecture Collection; **p18** Krause, Johansen/Archivo Iconografico, Sa/Corbis UK Ltd.; **p19** Gianni Dagli Orti/Corbis UK Ltd.; **p21** Erich Lessing /AKG - Images; **p22** Nimatallah/AKG – Images; **p23**t Gustavo Tomsich/Corbis UK Ltd., **p23**b Ladislav Janicek/Zefa/Corbis UK Ltd

Cover photograph: Axiom London

Illustrations by Katherine Baxter/Folio: **p5** (vignettes), **p9**, **p13**, **p16/17**, **p18**, **p20**; Martin Sanders/Beehive Illustration; **p4** (map).

Designed by Bigtop Design Ltd

CONTENTS

THE ANCIENT GREEK WORLD 4

SCARY SPHINX STRANGLER 6

BLOOD AND GUTS 8

BRINGING FIRE – AND TROUBLE 10

SURVIVAL SKILLS 12

YOU CAN'T CATCH ME! 14

THE QUEEN WHO RAN AWAY 16

MONEY, MAGIC AND MURDER 18

TOO CLOSE TO THE SUN 20

MONSTER IN A MAZE 22

HOW TO SAY NAMES 24

INDEX 24

THE ANCIENT GREEK WORLD

The Ancient Greeks were clever, busy people. They built cities and ships, travelled, traded, fought wars, played sport and made great discoveries.

The Greeks loved music, dancing – and stories. Their favourite stories were about heroes and monsters. Greek artists put pictures of them on all kinds of things, from big buildings to cooking pots.

Greek stories were fun. But they had a hidden message. They taught people how – or how not! – to behave. Today, we can still enjoy these stories, and they help us find out more about Ancient Greece.

As you read through this book, you can read some of the best Greek stories and discover how they were linked to real people's lives in Ancient Greece.

GREEK MONSTERS AND HEROES

Scary Sphinx Strangler

Thebes was a strong city, but its people were scared – because the gods had sent a monster to punish them. Its mouth was bloodstained, its huge wings hid the Sun, and its sharp claws grabbed greedily. It was the Sphinx – the Strangler!

The Sphinx swooped around, stopping passers-by. It asked them all the same riddle: "What walks on four legs, then two, then three?" They could not answer because they were too frightened. So the Sphinx killed and ate them!

Only Oedipus dared answer the Sphinx. It howled and snarled with fury. It had no more questions! Its power was gone! It fell to the ground and died.

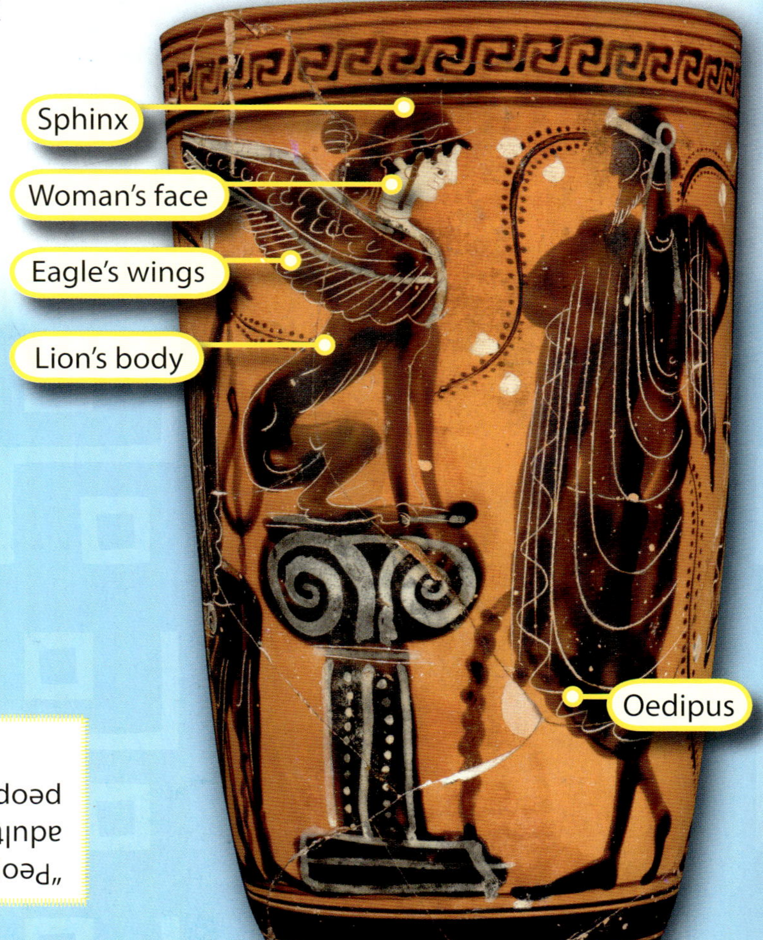

Oedipus's answer

"People! Babies crawl on all fours; adults walk on two legs; old people use walking sticks."

IN REAL LIFE ...

The Greeks believed they must give presents to their gods. If they forgot, the gods would punish them – just like they punished the Thebans by sending the Sphinx.

BLOOD AND GUTS

Baby Heracles was so strong he could strangle snakes. He grew up to be huge and handsome. He drove fast chariots, loved shooting and fighting, and fathered 50 sons.

But Heracles also went mad with rage. He liked blood and guts – he was dangerous! The gods said he must use his strength to help people, not harm them. He must drive away scary monsters and win precious treasures.

Heracles was a hero. He did all the gods asked! But then he died from poison. With a thunderbolt, the gods snatched him up to the sky to live with them forever.

IN REAL LIFE ...

Most Greek families were farmers. They had to work hard to survive. When hungry birds ate their crops, or wolves and bears killed their sheep, they would starve and die. Real, wild animals were just as dangerous as the magic monsters killed by Heracles.

BRINGING FIRE – AND TROUBLE

Was Prometheus a hero? The gods said "No! He stole our secrets!" Prometheus took fire – a new invention – from the gods. Then he gave it to men, because it would help them.

Angry gods sent an eagle to eat Prometheus alive. Then they made the first woman, to cause men trouble!

Her name was Pandora, and the gods gave her a beautiful box as a present. They warned her not to open it, but she peeked inside, just as they expected. Bad things flew out to trouble the world: death, anger, envy, cruelty, sickness and sorrow. Only hope stayed with her.

Tombstone showing Ancient Greek woman with a box of treasures.

Two Greek women washing clothes.

IN REAL LIFE ...

Greek men relied on women to run homes, raise children, cook food, make clothes, be good companions and offer wise advice. In spite of this, they often said that women – like Pandora – just could not be trusted.

That was not fair! Prometheus also disobeyed the gods, but Greek men admired him for his boldness and bravery.

SURVIVAL SKILLS

War-hero Odysseus was fighting far from home. He longed to see his family. But he angered Poseidon, god of the sea, who sent wind and waves to punish him.

Poseidon's storms kept Odysseus travelling for 10 long years. His journey was full of dangers. But Odysseus was quick-witted, and used clever tricks to survive.

At last, Odysseus reached home. But thieves were trying to steal his kingdom! He fought them, killed them, and lived happily ever after with his devoted wife, Penelope.

IN REAL LIFE …

Like Odysseus, Greek children needed survival skills. Boys learned by helping their fathers to run farms, build houses, sail ships, keep shops, or make useful things from wood, metal and pottery. Girls learned how to care for homes and families by helping their mothers.

Boys from rich families also went to school. Rich girls had lessons at home. Poor children never learned how to read or write.

YOU CAN'T CATCH ME!

Atalanta's parents wanted a boy, not a girl, so they left her out of doors to die. But Atalanta was rescued – by wild mountain bears! She grew fierce and strong and learned to fight, run fast and climb trees.

Atalanta killed a monster and became very famous. Many men fell in love with her. But she wanted a husband she could respect, and set a test to find the best partner. If a man could race against her and win, she would marry him!

Many men tried – and failed. Atalanta had them killed. But then Aphrodite, goddess of love, decided to help one young hero. His name was Milanion and she gave him three gold apples, all wonderfully shiny and beautiful. As he raced, Milanion dropped the apples – and Atalanta stopped running!

Atalanta married Milanion. Some say they had a son. But others say that Aphrodite was jealous and turned them into lions.

IN REAL LIFE ...

The Ancient Greeks loved sports. Their favourite sports were running, jumping, boxing, wrestling and throwing javelins (spears).

Greek cities held Games (sports festivals) to please their gods. Top athletes became superstars and won rich prizes.

We still use some Greek words for sport today.

English	**Greek**
athlete:	athletes = competitor
pentathlon:	pente = five + athlon = contest
stadium:	stadion = measurement used for racetracks
Olympic:	belonging to Olympia = place where Games were held to honour the god Zeus

THE QUEEN WHO RAN AWAY

Helen was as beautiful as the goddess of love. But her own love story was tragic. It brought death to many brave men and destroyed a fine city.

Helen lived in Sparta, home of famous Greek warriors. She was married to the king. But then she met Paris, a hero from Troy, and ran away with him.

The Greeks were outraged! Helen was their queen! They wanted her home again! They fought for ten years and then beat the Trojans. But it was a brutal victory.

Paris died fighting, but Helen survived, sad, sorry – and still beautiful.

A vase showing a beautiful Greek woman made around 500 BC.

Achilles (Greek) kills Hector (Trojan).

Paris (Trojan) kills Achilles (Greek).

Greeks hiding in Wooden Horse kill Trojans.

PROUD SPARTAN WARRIOR

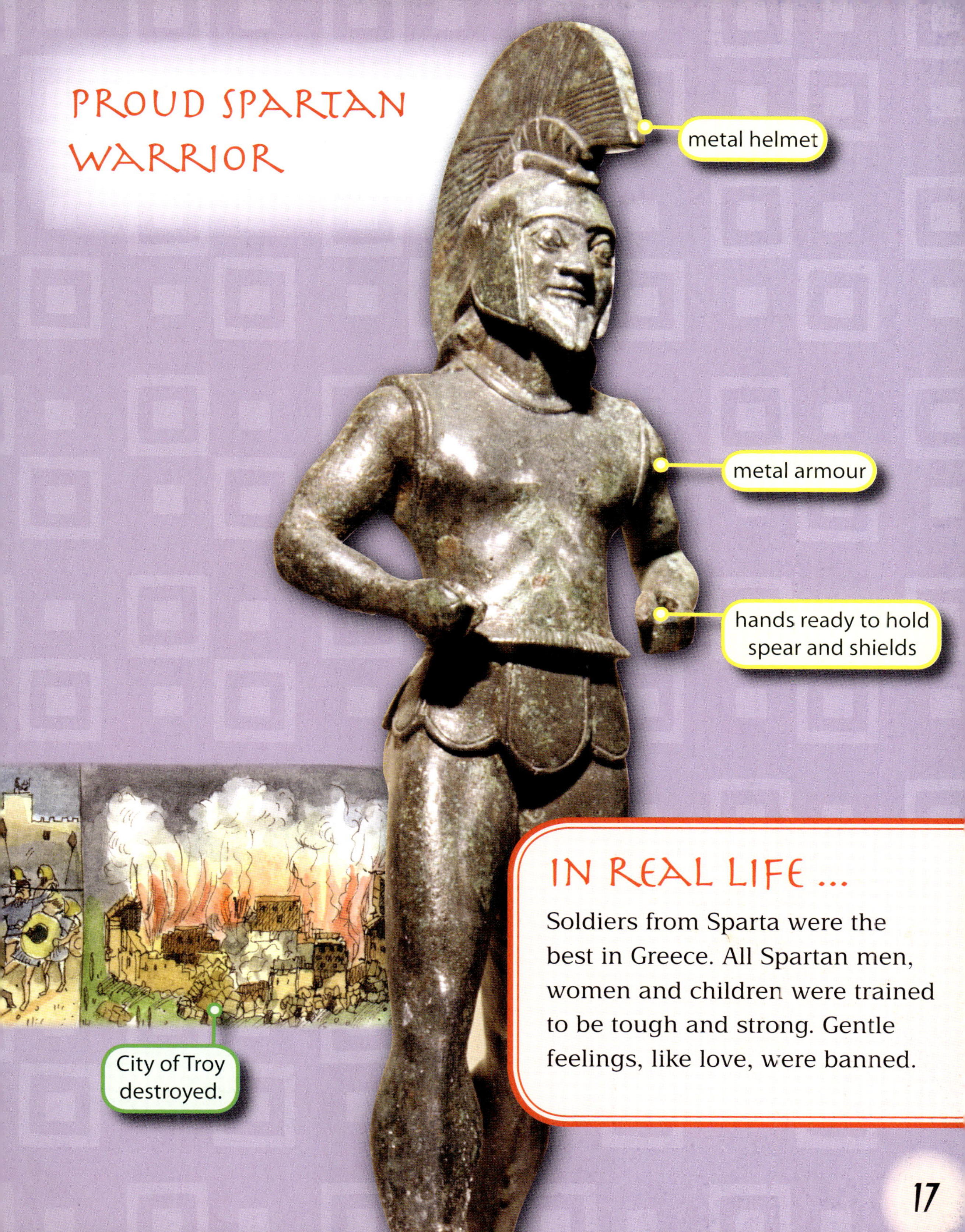

IN REAL LIFE ...

Soldiers from Sparta were the best in Greece. All Spartan men, women and children were trained to be tough and strong. Gentle feelings, like love, were banned.

MONEY, MAGIC AND MURDER

Even for a hero, Jason's life was strange. It was also very unhappy. Jason's greatest, strangest adventure was a long, exciting voyage to fetch the Golden Fleece. This was the skin of a magic ram – a rare, precious treasure. As Jason sailed along he was chased by giants, crushed by moving rocks and attacked by harpies (bird-monsters).

Jason found the Fleece. But it was in a magic tree, guarded by a dragon! A witch called Medea helped him get it. So Jason married her.

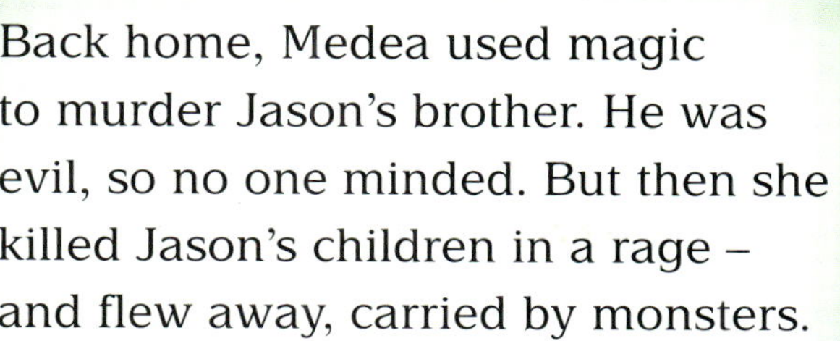

Back home, Medea used magic to murder Jason's brother. He was evil, so no one minded. But then she killed Jason's children in a rage – and flew away, carried by monsters.

Jason went to see his old ship and remember his past adventures. But the ship fell down, crushed him and killed him!

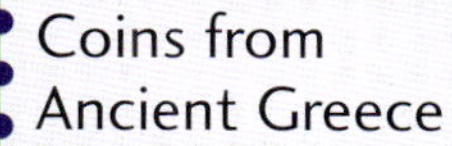

Coins from Ancient Greece

IN REAL LIFE ...

Greece is surrounded by the sea and the Greeks were great sailors, like Jason. They built fast wooden ships, powered by the wind and by men rowing.

Everywhere they travelled, Greek sailors liked to trade. They paid for treasures, like the Golden Fleece, with beautiful silver coins.

TOO CLOSE TO THE SUN

Designer, inventor, scientist, engineer – Daedalus was a superstar. But he quarrelled with the king, and rival inventors accused him of crimes. So Daedalus was put in prison, along with Icarus, his son.

Gloomily, Daedalus watched the birds outside. Then he had a brainwave. He would make wings like theirs, from feathers and wax, and fly away to freedom. Icarus tried the wings on, then flapped his arms. Yeeees!!!! He was flying!

Daedalus yelled, “Not too high!” and, “Mind the Sun – it’s hot!” but Icarus didn’t listen. The wax melted, his wings dropped off, and he drowned in the deep, dark sea.

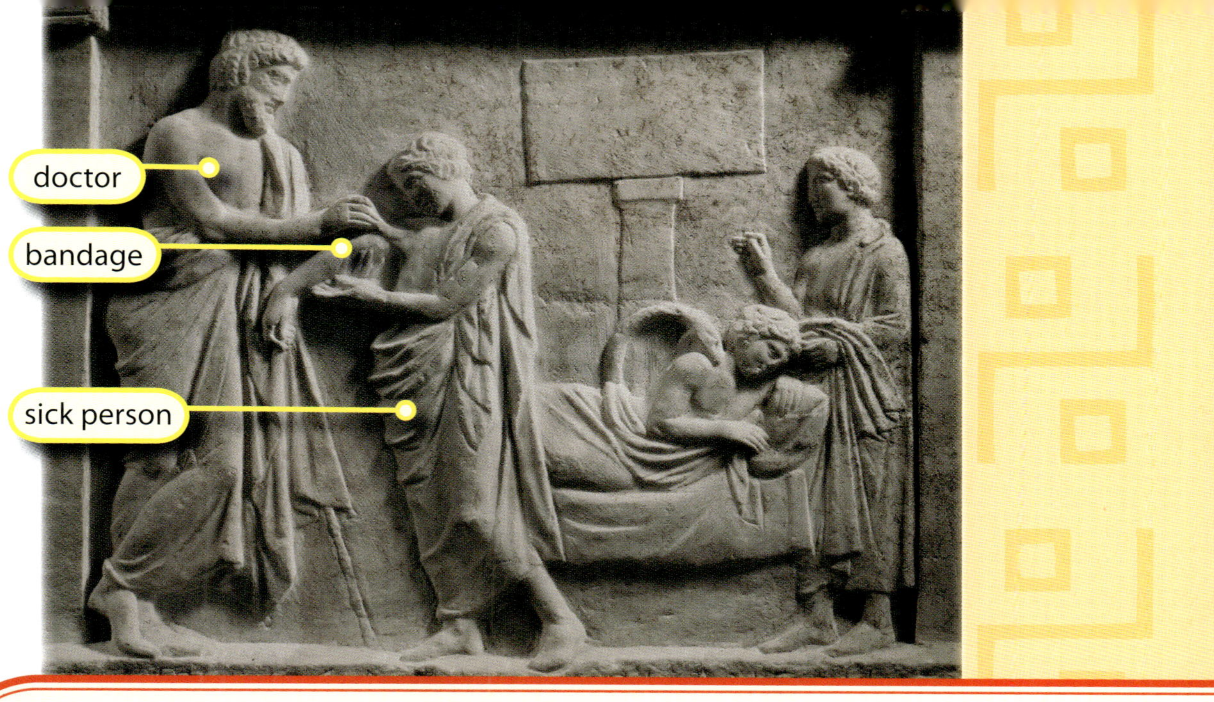

IN REAL LIFE ...

The Ancient Greeks were brilliant scientists, doctors and engineers. A few Greeks worried that new ideas might offend the gods, but clever people – like Daedalus – went on thinking and inventing. We still rely on Ancient Greek discoveries today. Here are some of the most famous:

Name	Job	Discovery or invention
Anaxagorus	astronomer	why the Moon shines
Archimedes	engineer	how things float
Aristarchus	astronomer	that the Earth goes round the Sun
Aristotle	philosopher	how to learn from what we see
Euclid	mathematician	how to measure
Heraclitus	philosopher	how to understand time and change
Hippocrates	doctor	scientific medicine
Plato	philosopher	how to judge what is real, good and true
Pythagoras	mathematician	an understanding of numbers
Pytheas	geographer/explorer	the size and shape of Europe and Africa
Socrates	philosopher	how to think and discuss clearly

MONSTER IN A MAZE

What had a man's body, bull's head, roaring voice – and ate children? The massive, miserable Minotaur! Savage and lonely, it lived in a deadly maze called the Labyrinth. Seven boys and seven girls were sent inside every year. They were never seen again.

Young Theseus was chosen to be Minotaur food. But he was determined not to die! He wound a huge ball of string, tied one end to the door and set off into the Labyrinth. He killed the Minotaur and came back alive – guided by the string he had trailed behind him!

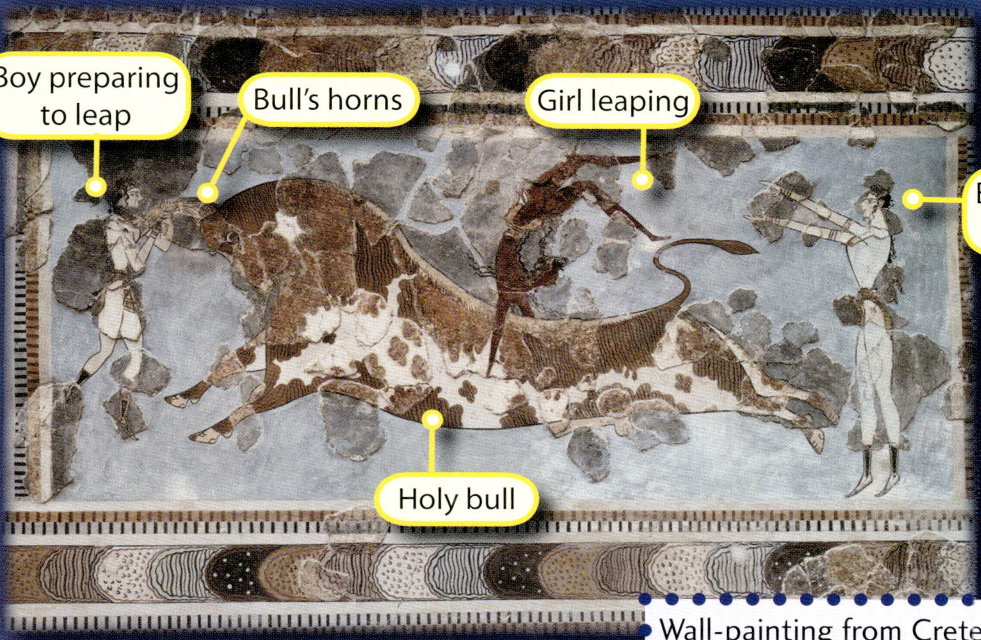

Boy preparing to leap

Bull's horns

Girl leaping

Boy waiting to catch

Holy bull

Wall-painting from Crete, 1500 BC

IN REAL LIFE ...

Long ago, the people of Crete thought that fierce bulls were holy. Young boys and girls played a dangerous sport as a way of worshipping them. They leapt over a bull's horns as it charged. Many must have died. The story of Theseus and the Minotaur was probably based on bull-leaping.

Theseus came from Athens. It became the richest and strongest city in Greece, with many fine buildings that still survive today.

HOW TO SAY NAMES

Aphrodite (Aff-roh-die-tee)
Atlalanta (At-ah-lan-tah)
Athens (Ath-ennz)
Calypso (Kal-ipp-so)
Charybdis (Kar-ibb-diss)
Circe (Sir-see OR Kir-kay)
Crete (Kreet)
Daedalus (Die-dal-uss)
Harpies (Harp-eez)
Heracles (Herr-ah-kleez)
Icarus (Ik-ar-uss)
Jason (Jay-son)
Labyrinth (Lab-urr-inth)
Medea (Med-ee-ah)
Milanion (Mill-ay-nee-on)
Minotaur (My-no-torr)
Odysseus (Odd-iss-ee-yoos)
Pandora (Pan-dorr-ah)
Paris (Pah-riss)
Penelope (Pen-ell-oh-pee)
Poseidon (Poz-eye-don)
Prometheus (Prom-ee-thee-uss)
Scylla (Sill-ah)
Sparta (Spar-tah)
Sphinx, the (Sfinx)
Thebes (Theebz)
Theseus (Thee-see-yoos)

INDEX

Aphrodite 14
Atlalanta 14
Athens 23
Bull-leaping 23
Calypso 13
Charybdis 13
Circe 13
Crete 23
Daedalus 20
Fire 10
Golden Fleece 18, 19
Harpies 18
Helen 16
Heracles 8, 9
Icarus 20
Jason 18, 19
Labyrinth 22
Medea 18
Milanion 14
Minotaur 22, 23
Odysseus 12, 13, 23
Pandora 10, 11
Paris 16
Penelope 12
Poseidon 12
Prometheus 6
Scylla 13
Sparta 17
Sphinx, the 6, 7
Thebes 6
Theseus 22, 23
Troy 16